NATIONAL GEOGRAPHIC

# On the Farm

Matthew Taylor

How many 🐖 live on the farm?

Two  live on the farm.

How many  live on the farm?

Three  live on the farm.

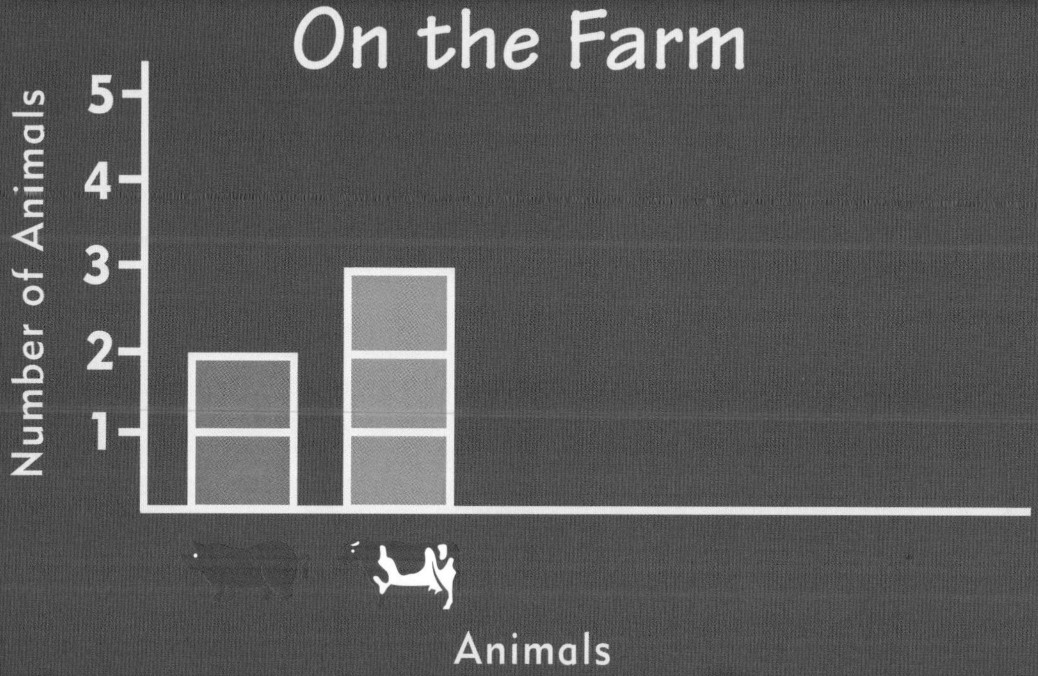

# How many  live on the farm?

Five  live on the farm.

How many live on the farm?

Four  live on the farm.

# How many live on the farm?

One [dog] lives on the farm.

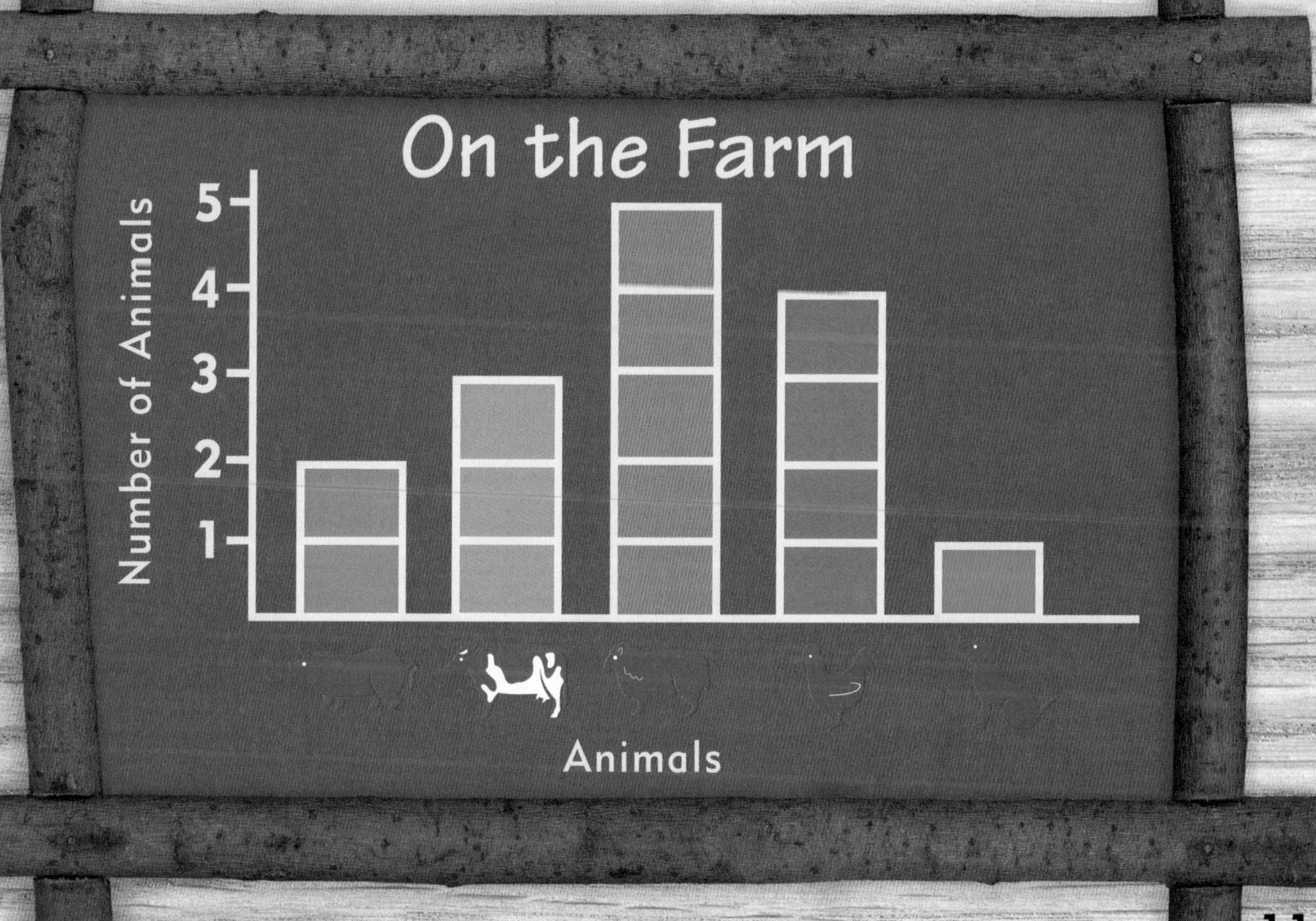

# How many animals live on the farm?